Specific Skill Series

Following Directions

Richard A. Boning

Fifth Edition

SRA/McGraw-Hill
Columbus, Ohio

Cover, Back Cover, ZEFA/Germany/The Stock Market

SRA/McGraw-Hill

A Division of The ***McGraw-Hill*** *Companies*

Printed in the United States of America.

Send all inquiries to:
SRA/McGraw-Hill
8787 Orion Place
Columbus, OH 43240-4027

FOURTH EDITION

ISBN 0-02-687931-X

9 WAL 05

4 5 6 IMP 97 96 95

To the Teacher

PURPOSE:
FOLLOWING DIRECTIONS is designed to develop skill in reading, understanding, and following instructions and directions. Proficiency in this basic skill is essential for success in every school subject and in nonacademic activities as well.

FOR WHOM:
The skill of FOLLOWING DIRECTIONS is developed through a series of books spanning ten levels (Picture, Preparatory, A, B, C, D, E, F, G, H). The Picture Level is for pupils who have not acquired a basic sight vocabulary. The Preparatory Level is for pupils who have a basic sight vocabulary but are not yet ready for the first-grade-level book. Books A through H are appropriate for pupils who can read on levels one through eight, respectively. **The use of the *Specific Skill Series Placement Test* is recommended to determine the appropriate level.**

THE NEW EDITION:
The fifth edition of the ***Specific Skill Series*** maintains the quality and focus that has distinguished this program for more than 25 years. A key element central to the program's success has been the unique nature of the reading selections. Nonfiction pieces about current topics have been designed to stimulate the interest of students, motivating them to use the comprehension strategies they have learned to further their reading. To keep this important aspect of the program intact, a percentage of the reading selections have been replaced in order to ensure the continued relevance of the subject material.

In addition, a significant percentage of the artwork in the program has been replaced to give the books a contemporary look. The cover photographs are designed to appeal to readers of all ages.

SESSIONS:
Short practice sessions are the most effective. It is desirable to have a practice session every day or every other day, using a few units each session.

SCORING:
Pupils should record their answers on the reproducible worksheets. The worksheets make scoring easier and provide uniform records of the pupils' work. Using worksheets also avoids consuming the exercise books.

To the Teacher

It is important for pupils to know how well they are doing. For this reason, units should be scored as soon as they have been completed. Then a discussion can be held in which pupils justify their choices. (The Integrated Language Activities, many of which are open-ended, do not lend themselves to an objective score; thus there are no answer keys for these pages.)

GENERAL INFORMATION ON *FOLLOWING DIRECTIONS*:

FOLLOWING DIRECTIONS focuses attention on four types of directions. The *testing and drilling* directions are like those in most textbooks and workbooks. Mastery of this type, so vital to school success, is stressed throughout FOLLOWING DIRECTIONS. The second type of direction is found in science books and involves *experimenting*. Such material requires the reader to find an answer to a problem or provides the reader with an example of practical application of a principle.

The third type of direction, *assembling*, deals with parts or ingredients and the order and way in which they are put together. Here the purpose is to make or create, rather than to solve a problem or demonstrate a principle.

Directions which tell how to do something are *performing* directions. They accent the steps in learning to do something new. The focus is on the performance rather than on the product.

SUGGESTED STEPS:

On levels A-H, pupils read the information above the first line. Then they answer the questions *below* this line. (Pupils are *not* to respond in writing to information *above* the first line; they are only to study it. Pupils should not write or mark anything in this book.) On the Picture Level, pupils tell if a picture correctly follows the directions. On the Preparatory Level, pupils tell which picture out of two correctly follows the directions.

Additional information on using FOLLOWING DIRECTIONS with pupils will be found in the **Specific Skill Series Teacher's Manual**.

RELATED MATERIALS:

Specific Skill Series Placement Tests, which enable the teacher to place pupils at their appropriate levels in each skill, are available for the Elementary (Pre-1–6) and Midway (4–8) grade levels.

About This Book

Following directions is an important part of your life. At home, your parents may say, “Put away your things.” In school, your teacher may say, “Write your name at the top of your paper.” On the street, the crossing guard may say, “Do not cross yet.”

Following directions is like trying to find your way with a map. If you follow the map correctly, you will get where you want to go. If you make a mistake, you will get lost.

It is important to understand directions. It is important to follow them correctly.

Think about directions carefully. Ask yourself questions like these: What do the directions tell me to do? Do I understand all the words in the directions? Should I do one thing before I do another?

In this book, you will read directions that tell you to do something. You are **not** to follow the directions. Instead, you will answer questions about the directions.

For questions 1 and 2, you will decide what the directions say to do.

For question 3 you will decide if someone followed the directions. Think about the directions. Think about what the picture shows. Then answer the question, “Is it right?” Choose **Yes** if the picture shows the directions followed correctly. Choose **No** if the picture shows the directions **not** followed correctly.

UNIT 1

DIRECTIONS:

Find the sun. Draw a line under it.

1. You are to look for the—

   (A) boat

   (B) sun

   (C) flower

2. You are to make—

   (A) a line

   (B) an X

   (C) a circle

3. Is it right? **(A) Yes** **(B) No**

UNIT 2

DIRECTIONS:

Draw a line over the cloud.

---

1. You are to look for the—

   (A) cloud

   (B) apple

   (C) birds

---

2. You are to make a—

   (A) picture

   (B) line

   (C) circle

---

3. Is it right? **(A) Yes** **(B) No**

UNIT 3

DIRECTIONS:

Draw a circle around the black rabbit.

---

1. You are to look for the—

   (A) apple

   (B) black rabbit

   (C) white rabbit

2. You are to make—

   (A) a line

   (B) a circle

   (C) an X

3. Is it right? **(A) Yes** **(B) No**

UNIT 4

DIRECTIONS:

Find the puppy that is sleeping. Put an X on it.

1. You are to look for a puppy that is—

    (A) white

    (B) sleeping

    (C) running

2. You are to make—

    (A) an X

    (B) a circle

    (C) a line

3. Is it right? **(A) Yes** **(B) No**

UNIT 5

DIRECTIONS:

Find the picture of the goat. Put a line under it.

---

1. You are to look for the—

   (A) man

   (B) goat

   (C) hen

---

2. Your line must be—

   (A) on it

   (B) in it

   (C) under it

---

3. Is it right? **(A) Yes** **(B) No**

UNIT 6

DIRECTIONS:

Draw a line from the train to the penny.

---

1. You are to look for the—

   (A) store and penny

   (B) store and train

   (C) train and penny

---

2. You are to make—

   (A) a circle

   (B) a line

   (C) an X

---

3. Is it right? **(A) Yes** **(B) No**

UNIT 7

DIRECTIONS:

Find the horse. Put a line under it.

1. You are to look for the—

   (A) doll

   (B) pig

   (C) horse

2. You are to make—

   (A) a line

   (B) an X

   (C) a circle

3. Is it right? **(A) Yes** **(B) No**

UNIT 8

DIRECTIONS:

Draw a line from the elephant to the kitten.

1. You are to look for the elephant and—

   (A) book

   (B) kitten

   (C) horse

2. The line must go from the elephant to the—

   (A) book

   (B) kitten

   (C) horse

3. Is it right? **(A) Yes** **(B) No**

UNIT 9

DIRECTIONS:

Find the shoe. Put an X on it.

---

1. You are to look for the—

   (A) shoe

   (B) coat

   (C) puppy

---

2. Your X is to be—

   (A) under it

   (B) on it

   (C) over it

---

3. Is it right?  **(A) Yes**  **(B) No**

UNIT 10

DIRECTIONS:

Draw a circle around the white car.

---

1. You are to find the—

   (A) black car

   (B) white car

   (C) white cat

2. You are to draw—

   (A) a circle

   (B) a line

   (C) an X

3. Is it right? **(A) Yes** **(B) No**

UNIT 11

DIRECTIONS:

Put a line over the barn.

1. You are to look for the—

   (A) barn

   (B) window

   (C) black hen

2. You are to make—

   (A) a circle around it

   (B) a line over it

   (C) an X on it

3. Is it right?  **(A) Yes**  **(B) No**

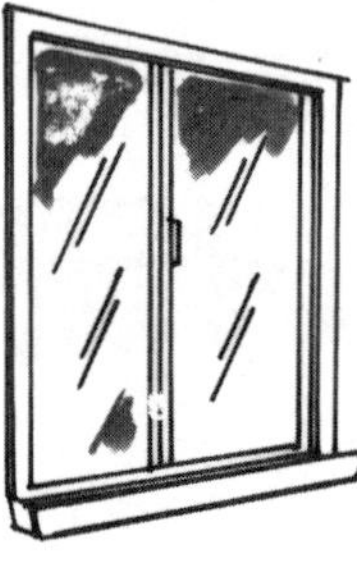

UNIT 12

DIRECTIONS:

Make a circle around the three cows.

---

1. You are to look for—

   (A) the big cow

   (B) three cows

   (C) the little cow

---

2. You are to make—

   (A) a line under

   (B) a circle around

   (C) an X on

---

3. Is it right? **(A) Yes** **(B) No**

A. Exercising Your Skill

Look at the animals. Follow the directions.

1. Draw the tail of the animal that is big.
2. Draw the ears of the animal that can hop.
3. Draw the head of the animal that can fly.

B. Expanding Your Skill

Draw an animal this way.

1. Draw a big circle.
2. Draw a little circle on top of the big circle.
3. Make two little ears on the top circle.
4. Add a long tail to the bottom circle.

Now you have a cat! Color your cat. Think of a name for your cat. Write the name under the cat.

C. Exploring Language

Make up a funny animal. Tell how to draw it. Copy these directions. Fill in the blanks.

Draw my funny animal. Give it a ____ body. Put ____ legs on it. Draw a ____ head. Add ____ eyes. Color them ____ . My animal has ____ teeth and a ____ nose. It likes to wear ____ . Draw that, too.

D. Expressing Yourself

Make a funny monster with a friend. You each need a sheet of paper. Follow the directions.

1. Fold your paper in half like this.

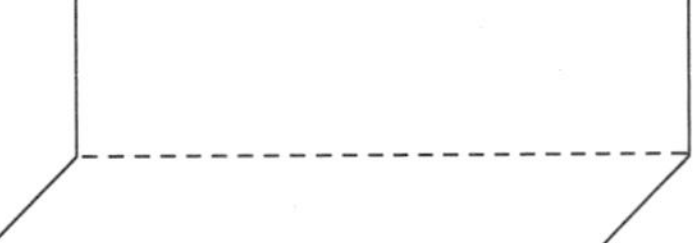

2. Hold the paper so the fold is on the bottom. Draw the head and neck of a funny monster. Make them end near the fold. Don't let your friend see!
3. Turn the paper over so the fold is at the top. Swap papers with your friend.
4. Now you have your friend's paper. Draw the body and legs of your monster. Make the body start near the top fold.
5. Unfold the paper to see a funny monster!

UNIT 13

DIRECTIONS:

Put an X on the big bed.

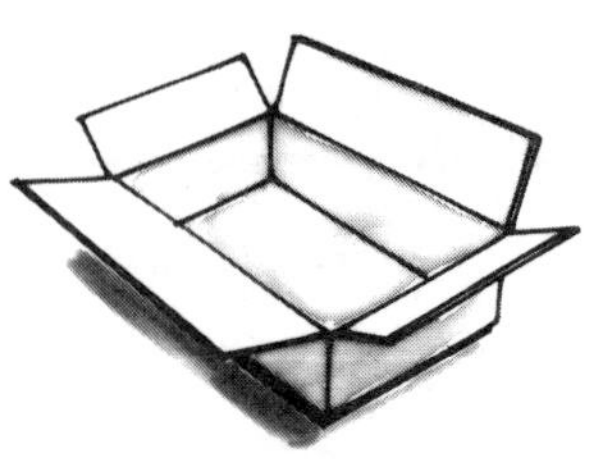
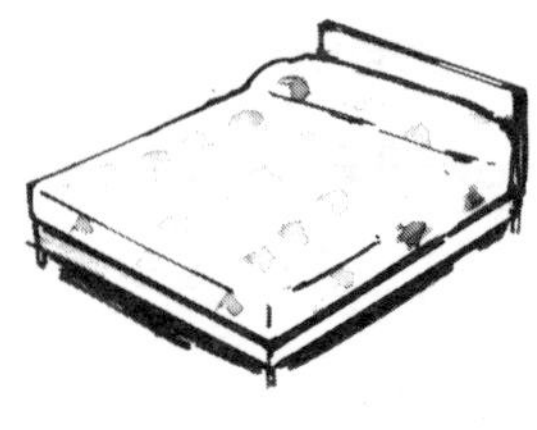

1. You are to look for the—

   (A) box

   (B) bed

   (C) kitten

2. You are to put the X—

   (A) on it

   (B) over it

   (C) under it

3. Is it right? **(A) Yes** **(B) No**

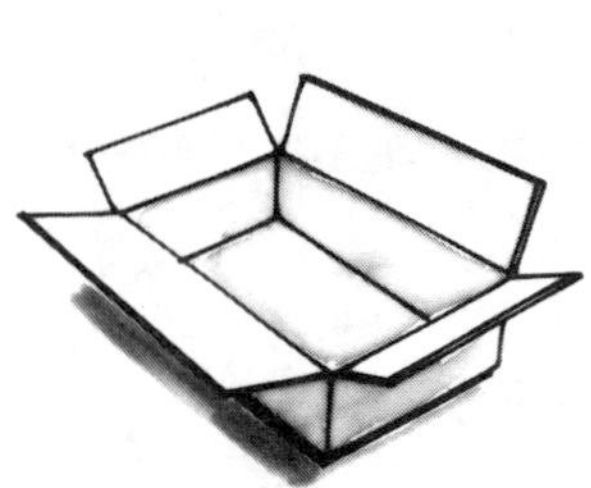
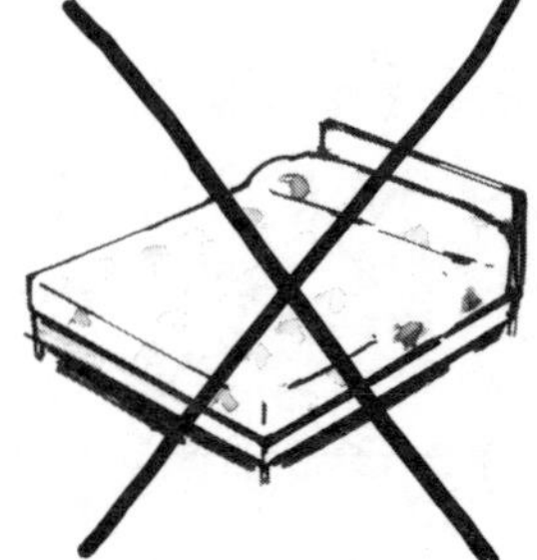

UNIT 14

DIRECTIONS:

Find the picture of the baby elephant. Make a line under it.

1. You are to look for the—

   (A) truck

   (B) big elephant

   (C) baby elephant

2. You are to put a line—

   (A) under it

   (B) on it

   (C) over it

3. Is it right? **(A) Yes** **(B) No**

UNIT 15

DIRECTIONS:

Draw a line under the house.

---

1. You are to look for the—

   (A) toy

   (B) house

   (C) saw

---

2. You must make—

   (A) a circle

   (B) a line

   (C) an X

---

3. Is it right? **(A) Yes** **(B) No**

UNIT 16

DIRECTIONS:

Find the horse that is running. Put a line under it.

1. You are to look for the horse that is—

   (A) running

   (B) walking

   (C) sleeping

2. Your line must be—

   (A) under the horse

   (B) on the horse

   (C) over the horse

3. Is it right? **(A) Yes** **(B) No**

UNIT 17

DIRECTIONS:

Find the big cake. Put an X under it.

---

1. You are to look for the—

   (A) little cake

   (B) big cake

   (C) big coat

---

2. You are to make an X—

   (A) on it

   (B) over it

   (C) under it

---

3. Is it right? **(A) Yes** **(B) No**

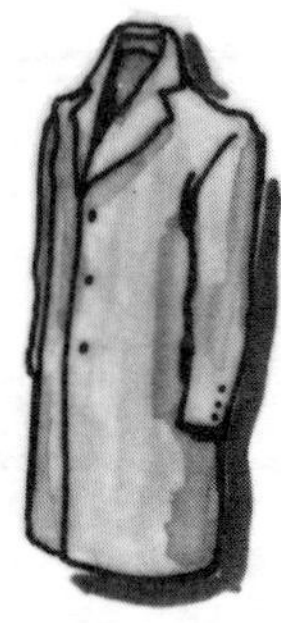

UNIT 18

DIRECTIONS:

Put a line under the girl who is jumping.

---

1. You are to find the girl who is—

    (A) jumping

    (B) running

    (C) talking

---

2. You are to make a line—

    (A) on her

    (B) under her

    (C) after her

---

3. Is it right?  **(A) Yes**  **(B) No**

UNIT 19

DIRECTIONS:

Find the picture of the little hill. Put a line under it.

1. You are to look for the—
   (A) big hill
   (B) little hill
   (C) airplane

2. You are to put a line—
   (A) under it
   (B) over it
   (C) on it

3. Is it right? **(A) Yes** **(B) No**

UNIT 20

DIRECTIONS:

Find the black kitten. Put a line under it.

1. You are to look for the—

   (A) black kitten

   (B) white kitten

   (C) big hat

2. You are to make—

   (A) an X

   (B) a circle

   (C) a line

3. Is it right? **(A) Yes** **(B) No**

UNIT 21

DIRECTIONS:

Find the big balloon. Put two lines over it.

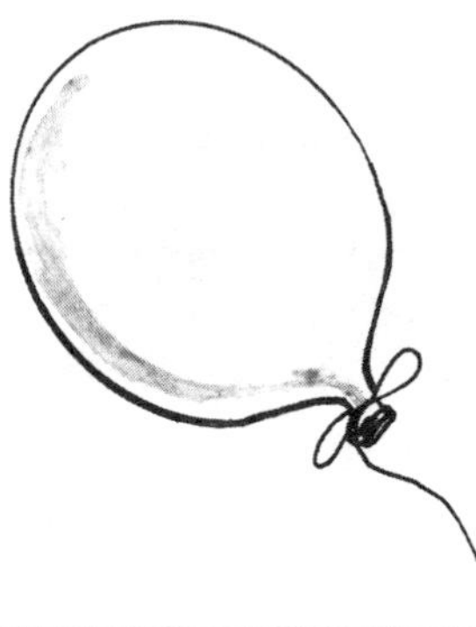
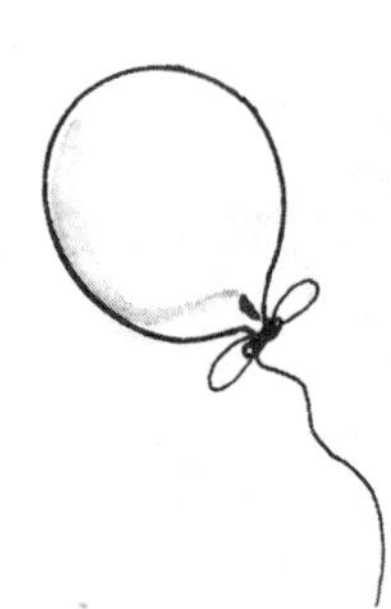

1. You are to look for the—

   (A) big balloon

   (B) little balloon

   (C) street

2. You are to make—

   (A) one line

   (B) two lines

   (C) one circle

3. Is it right? **(A) Yes** **(B) No**

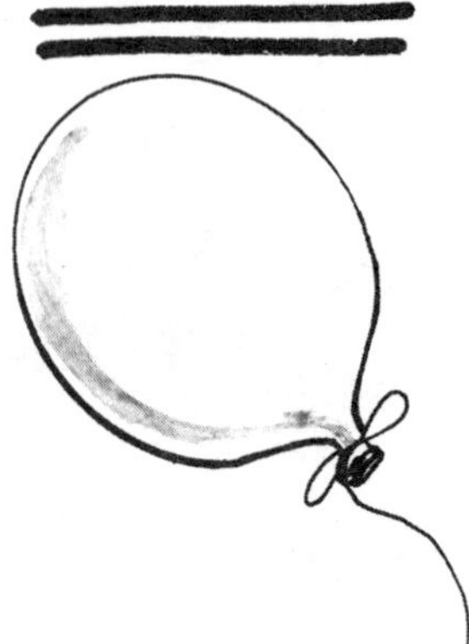

DIRECTIONS:

Put a line over the house.

1. You are to find the—

(A) school

(B) rainbow

(C) house

2. Make a line—

(A) over it

(B) under it

(C) on it

3. Is it right? **(A) Yes** **(B) No**

UNIT 23

DIRECTIONS:

Draw a line from the chair to the clown.

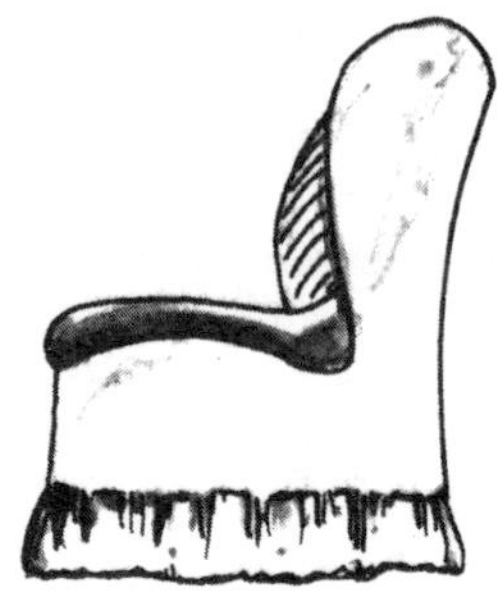

1. You are to find the chair and the—

   (A) clown

   (B) corn

   (C) book

2. The line should go from the chair to the—

   (A) book

   (B) corn

   (C) clown

3. Is it right? **(A) Yes** **(B) No**

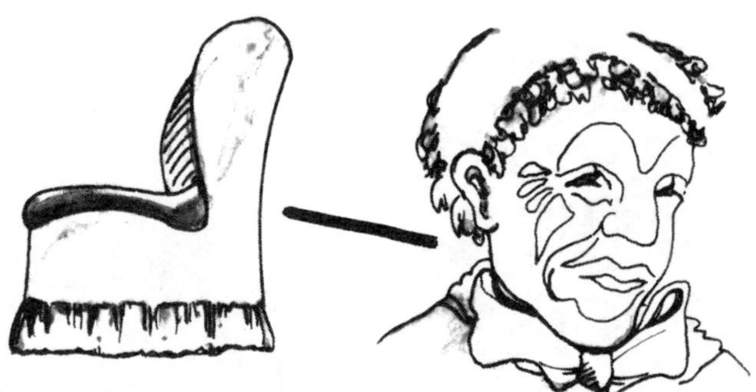

UNIT 24

DIRECTIONS:

Make a line from the rabbit to the duck.

---

1. You are to look for the—

   (A) rabbit and duck

   (B) rabbit and mouse

   (C) duck and mouse

---

2. You are to make—

   (A) a circle

   (B) an X

   (C) a line

---

3. Is it right? **(A) Yes** **(B) No**

on

in

under

A. Exercising Your Skill

Draw a picture of the nest.
Draw 3 little eggs in it.
Draw a mother bird on it.
Draw a tree branch under it.

B. Expanding Your Skill

Work with a partner to make a picture. Use the direction words below. Have the picture show what each word means. For example, to show the word under, you might draw a picture of a dog hiding under a bed.

over **under** **on** **beside**

Show the picture to your classmates. Ask them to tell you where things are in the picture.

C. Exploring Language

Read the story below. Add the missing words on your paper. Find them in the box.

on	under	around	over	in

You can go for a pony ride. The pony is ____ the barn. Put the saddle ____ the pony's back. But first put this blanket ____ the saddle. Ride the pony ____ this track. Do not try to jump ____ anything. Have fun!

D. Expressing Yourself

Do one of these things.

1. Make a word picture. The picture should look like what the word means. Here are two examples.

J U M P **FAT**

2. Work with classmates. Make up a story with them. It can be like the one about the pony ride. It can be about anything. Use these words in the story: **on, off, under, over.**

UNIT 25

DIRECTIONS:

Find the kite. Put a line under the kite.

---

1. You are to look for the—

   (A) boy

   (B) kite

   (C) duck

---

2. You are to make—

   (A) a line

   (B) an X

   (C) a circle

---

3. Is it right? **(A) Yes** **(B) No**

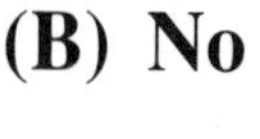

UNIT 26

DIRECTIONS:

Draw a line from the nest to the bird.

1. You are to look for the—

   (A) nest and tree

   (B) nest and bird

   (C) bird and tree

2. You are to make a—

   (A) line

   (B) picture

   (C) circle

3. Is it right? **(A) Yes** **(B) No**

UNIT 27

DIRECTIONS:

Make an X on the rabbit.

1. You are to find the—

   (A) house

   (B) rabbit

   (C) car

2. You are to make—

   (A) an X

   (B) a line

   (C) a circle

3. Is it right? **(A) Yes** **(B) No**

UNIT 28

DIRECTIONS:

Draw a line from the duck to the water.

---

1. You are to find the—

   (A) duck and wagon

   (B) wagon and water

   (C) duck and water

---

2. You are to make—

   (A) a line

   (B) a circle

   (C) an X

---

3. Is it right? **(A) Yes** **(B) No**

UNIT 29

DIRECTIONS:

Make a line from the glass to the table.

---

1. You are to look for the—

   (A) glass and the table

   (B) glass and the pot

   (C) pot and the table

---

2. You are to make—

   (A) an X

   (B) a circle

   (C) a line

---

3. Is it right? **(A) Yes** **(B) No**

UNIT 30

DIRECTIONS:

Find the black balloon. Put a line under it.

1. You are to look for the—

   (A) white balloon

   (B) black balloon

   (C) hen

2. You are to make—

   (A) a line

   (B) a circle

   (C) an X

3. Is it right? **(A) Yes** **(B) No**

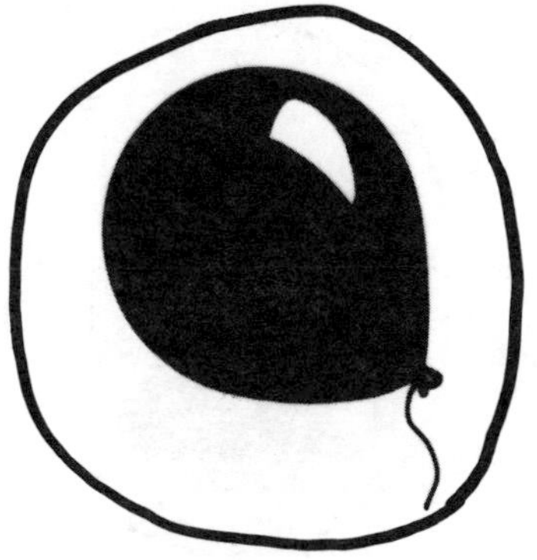  

UNIT 31

DIRECTIONS:

Put an X on the TV.

 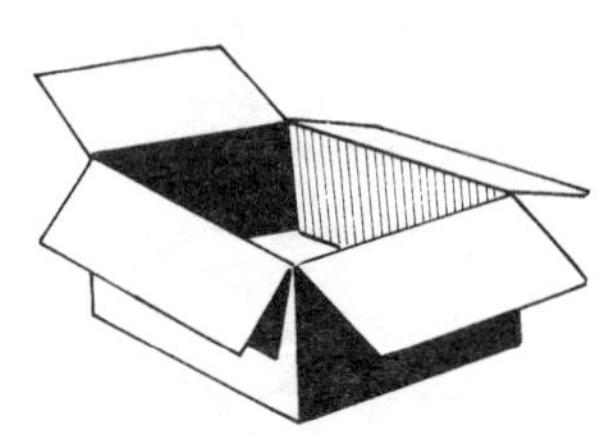 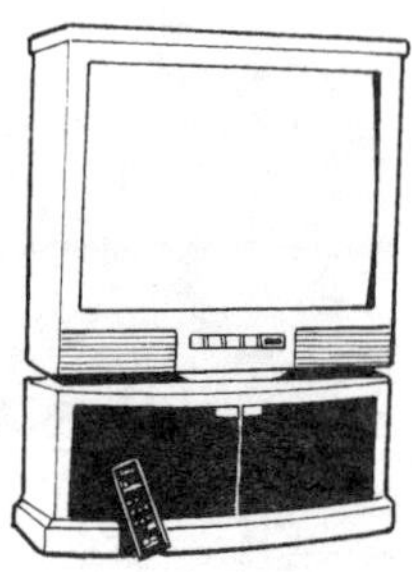

---

1. You are to find the—

   (A) TV

   (B) bear

   (C) box

---

2. You are to make—

   (A) a line

   (B) a circle

   (C) an X

---

3. Is it right? **(A) Yes** **(B) No**

 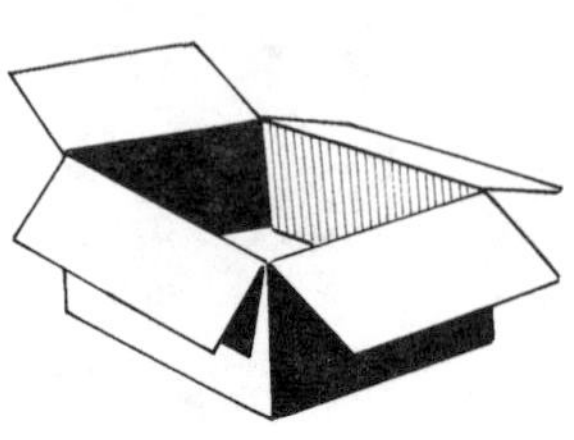 

UNIT 32

DIRECTIONS:

Find the school. Put a line under it.

1. You are to look for the—

   (A) house

   (B) school

   (C) store

2. You are to make—

   (A) an X

   (B) a circle

   (C) a line

3. Is it right? **(A) Yes** **(B) No**

UNIT 33

DIRECTIONS:

Find the picture of food. Put an X on it.

---

1. You are to look for the—

   (A) food

   (B) bag

   (C) eyes

---

2. You are to put—

   (A) an X on it

   (B) a circle around it

   (C) a line under it

---

3. Is it right? **(A) Yes** **(B) No**

UNIT 34

DIRECTIONS:

Find the star. Put a circle around it.

1. You are to look for the—

   (A) star

   (B) letters

   (C) tire

2. You are to make a circle—

   (A) under it

   (B) over it

   (C) around it

3. Is it right? **(A) Yes** **(B) No**

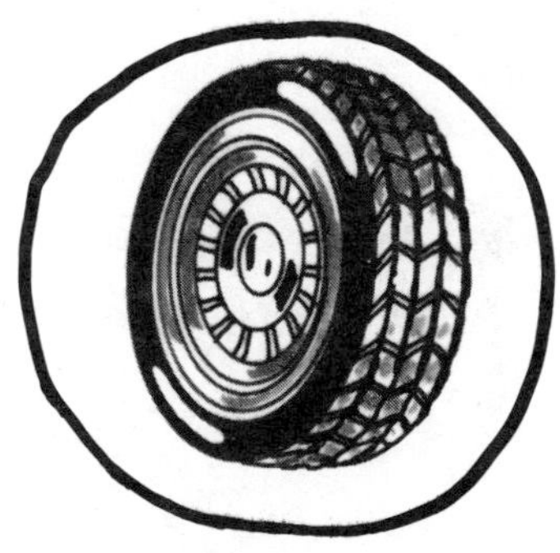

UNIT 35

DIRECTIONS:

Find the bat. Put a circle around it.

---

1. You are to find the—

   (A) food

   (B) bat

   (C) shoe

2. You are to make—

   (A) a line

   (B) a circle

   (C) an X

3. Is it right?  **(A) Yes**  **(B) No**

UNIT 36

DIRECTIONS:

Find the picture of the airplane. Put two lines over it.

---

1. You are to look for the—

   (A) car

   (B) airplane

   (C) train

---

2. You are to make—

   (A) two lines

   (B) a line

   (C) an X

---

3. Is it right? **(A) Yes** **(B) No**

UNIT 37

DIRECTIONS:

Draw a line from the girl to the dog.

---

1. You are to look for the—

   (A) house and dog

   (B) girl and house

   (C) girl and dog

---

2. You are to make—

   (A) an X

   (B) a circle

   (C) a line

---

3. Is it right? **(A) Yes** **(B) No**

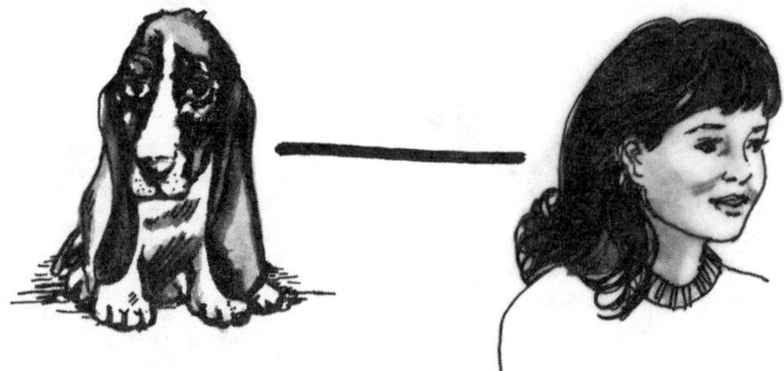

UNIT 38

DIRECTIONS:

Find the hat. Put a circle around it.

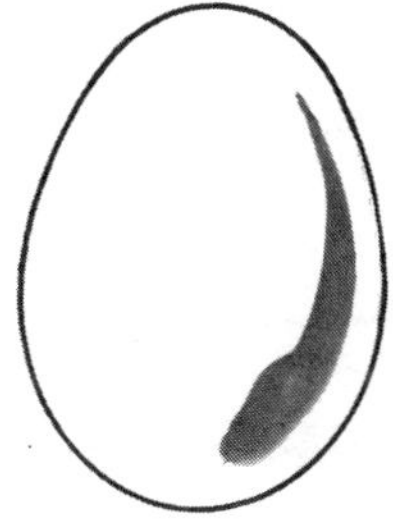  

---

1. You are to look for the—

   (A) egg

   (B) hat

   (C) nest

---

2. You are to make—

   (A) a line

   (B) an X

   (C) a circle

---

3. Is it right? **(A) Yes** **(B) No**

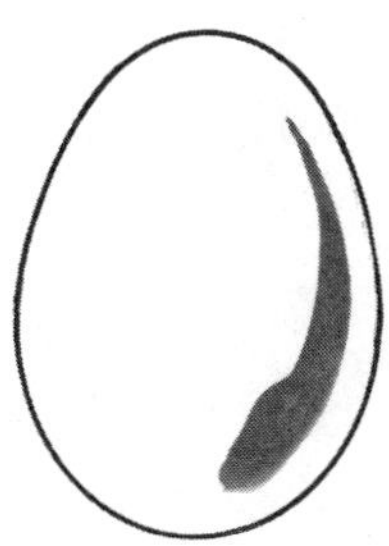  

A. Exercising Your Skill

Look at the pictures. Follow the directions.

turtle

bee

wagon

1. Write the name of the thing that can fly. Make the name yellow.
2. Write the name of the thing that you ride in. Make the name red.
3. Write the name of the thing that can swim. Make the name green.

B. Expanding Your Skill

Work with a friend. Follow these directions.

1. Draw two things that live in the sea. Make one big and one small.
2. Draw something that will fit in your pocket. Make it blue.
3. Draw something that is green and can grow.

C. Exploring Language

Do all of these things. Use your own paper.

1. Write the names of three things you can eat. Circle the one you like best.
2. Write the names of three things that make sounds. Put an X on the loudest one.
3. Write the names of three toys. Put a box around the smallest one.

D. Expressing Yourself

Do one of these things.

1. See if you can give good directions. First, clear an area in the classroom. Put down sheets of paper here and there. Take a classmate to one side of the area. Ask the classmate to close his or her eyes. Tell the classmate how to get across the area without stepping on a paper.
2. Take turns giving directions with a friend. First, draw something on your paper. Don't let your friend see it! Now give your friend directions for how to draw the same thing. But don't tell what the thing is! Do the two pictures look anything alike?

UNIT 39

DIRECTIONS:

Find the fan. Draw a circle around it.

---

1. You are to look for the—

(A) fish

(B) fan

(C) train

---

2. You are to make—

(A) a circle

(B) an X

(C) a line

---

3. Is it right? **(A) Yes** **(B) No**

UNIT 40

DIRECTIONS:

Find the pocket. Put a line over it.

---

1. You are to find the—

   (A) fire

   (B) pocket

   (C) window

---

2. You are to draw a line—

   (A) under it

   (B) over it

   (C) on it

---

3. Is it right?  **(A) Yes**  **(B) No**

 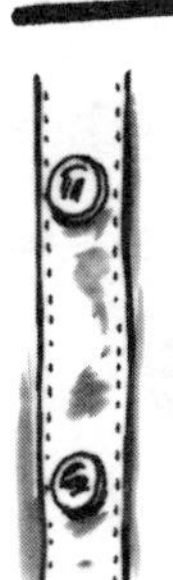  

UNIT 41

DIRECTIONS:

Draw a line from the chicken to the squirrel.

---

1. You are to find the chicken and the—

   (A) squirrel

   (B) bear

   (C) puppy

---

2. You will draw—

   (A) a circle

   (B) two lines

   (C) one line

---

3. Is it right? **(A) Yes** **(B) No**

UNIT 42

DIRECTIONS:

Draw a line from Mother to Father.

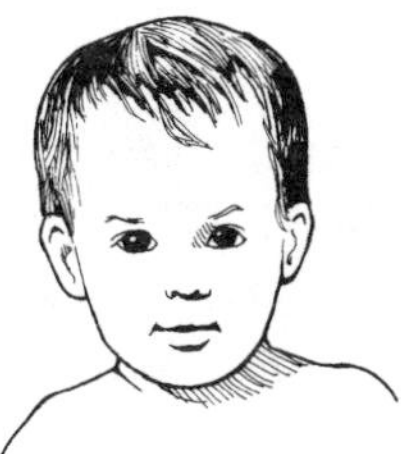

---

1. You are to find Father and—

   (A) house

   (B) baby

   (C) Mother

---

2. The line must go from Mother to—

   (A) Mother

   (B) baby

   (C) Father

---

3. Is it right? **(A) Yes** **(B) No**

UNIT 43

DIRECTIONS:

Find the table. Put a circle around it.

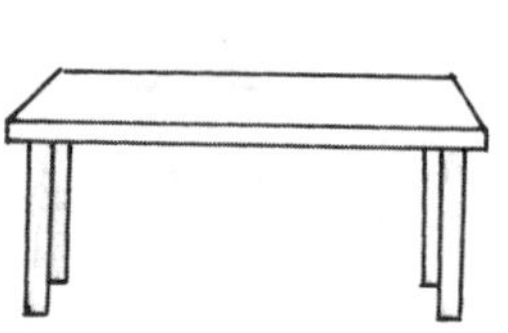  

---

1. You are to look for the—

   (A) hat

   (B) toys

   (C) table

---

2. You are to make—

   (A) a circle

   (B) a line

   (C) an X

---

3. Is it right? **(A) Yes** **(B) No**

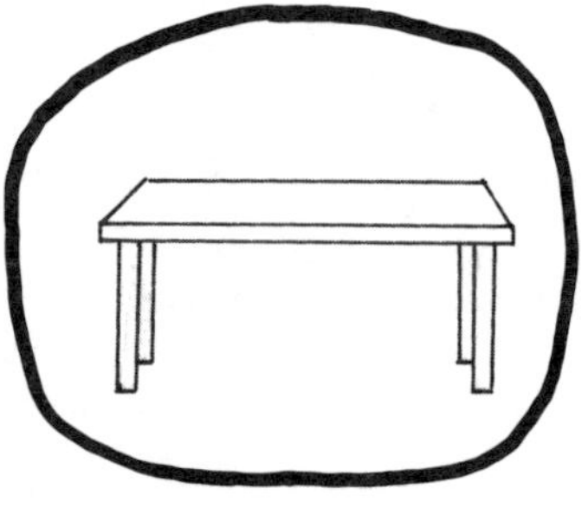  

UNIT 44

DIRECTIONS:

Find the biggest turtle. Put a circle around it.

1. You are to find the—

   (A) biggest turtle

   (B) littlest turtle

   (C) two turtles

2. You are to make—

   (A) a line

   (B) a circle

   (C) an X

3. Is it right?  **(A) Yes**  **(B) No**

UNIT 45

DIRECTIONS:

Put a circle around two of the cookies.

---

1. You are to find—

   (A) one cookie

   (B) two cookies

   (C) one book

---

2. You are to make—

   (A) a circle

   (B) an X

   (C) a line

---

3. Is it right? **(A) Yes** **(B) No**

UNIT 46

DIRECTIONS:

Put an X on the truck. Make a circle around the egg.

---

1. You are to find the—

   (A) truck and egg

   (B) truck and sun

   (C) egg and sun

---

2. You are to make—

   (A) an X and a circle

   (B) a line and an X

   (C) a line and a circle

---

3. Is it right? **(A) Yes** **(B) No**

  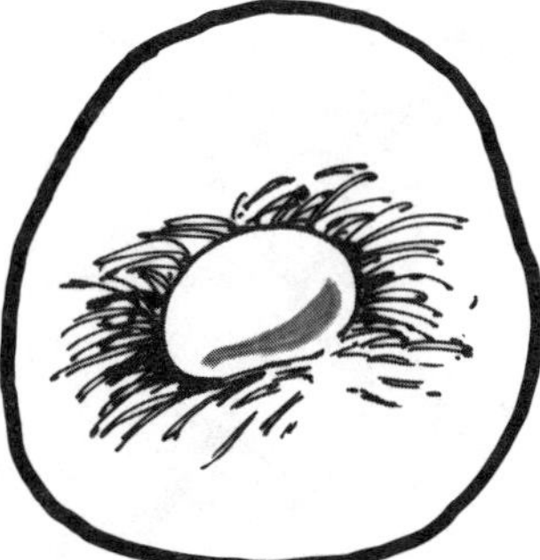

UNIT 47

DIRECTIONS:

Put an X on the bag. Make a line under the fire.

1. You are to find the—

   (A) bag and fire

   (B) bag and bee

   (C) fire and bee

2. You are to make an X and—

   (A) a circle

   (B) a line

   (C) two lines

3. Is it right? **(A) Yes** **(B) No**

UNIT 48

DIRECTIONS:

Put an X on the tree. Make a circle around the coat.

---

1. You are to look for the—

   (A) tree and apple

   (B) apple and coat

   (C) tree and coat

---

2. You are to make—

   (A) an X and a line

   (B) a circle and a line

   (C) an X and a circle

---

3. Is it right? **(A) Yes** **(B) No**

  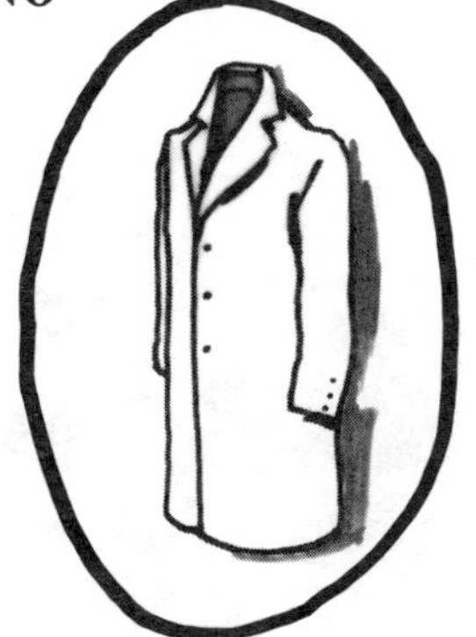

UNIT 49

DIRECTIONS:

Put a line under the saw. Put two lines under the bird.

1. You are to find the saw and—

   (A) rabbit

   (B) squirrel

   (C) bird

2. You must make one line under the—

   (A) squirrel

   (B) bird

   (C) saw

3. Is it right? **(A) Yes** **(B) No**

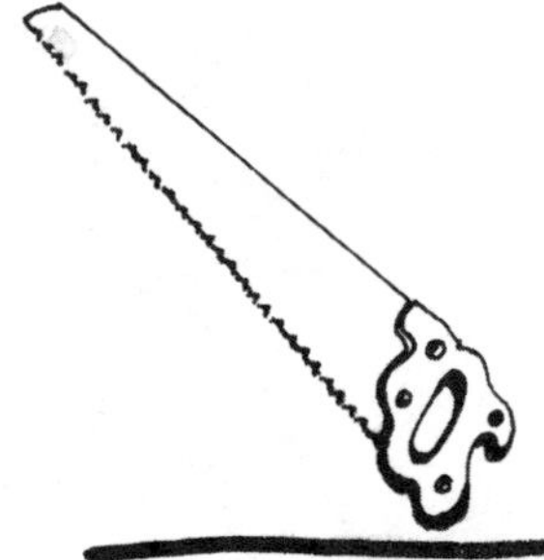

UNIT 50

DIRECTIONS:

Put an X on the cat and a line under the mouse.

1. You are to look for the—

   (A) cat and mouse

   (B) cat and dog

   (C) cat and tree

2. You are to make an X and—

   (A) a circle

   (B) two lines

   (C) a line

3. Is it right? **(A) Yes** **(B) No**

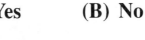

apple **shoe** **table**

A. Exercising Your Skill

Look at the pictures. Then follow the directions.

1. Find the thing that has legs. Write its name.
2. Find the thing that has a skin. Write its name.
3. Find the thing that has a heel and toe. Write its name.

B. Expanding Your Skill

Read the words with a partner. See if you can tell what the words are about. But don't say it!

It has a face.
It has two hands.
It cannot talk.
But it can tell time.
What is it?

Now draw a picture of what it is. Show the picture to your partner. Did you get it right?

C. Exploring Language

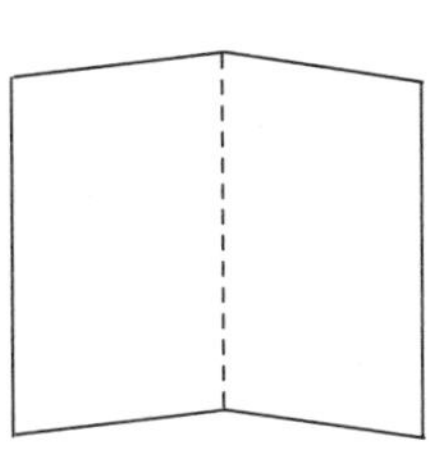

Fold a sheet of paper in half.
Make the fold go up and down.
Lay the paper flat.

Draw these two things at the top.

1. Draw an eye on the left side.
2. Draw an ear on the right side.

Now do these two things:

1. Under the eye, write the names of three things you can see.
2. Under the ear, write the names of three things you can hear.

D. Expressing Yourself

Do one of these things.

1. Make a mask. Use a brown paper bag. Draw or cut out things on the mask. Put the mask on. Ask your classmates if they can tell what you are.
2. Draw a stick person. What job can the person do? Add the clothes the person needs for this job. Add the things the person needs to do the job. Show your picture to your classmates. See if they can tell what job the person can do.